D1334520

Movie
MAGIC

FANTASTIC BEASTS
THE CRIMES OF
GRINDELWALD™

Movie MAGIC

PENGUIN BOOKS

CONTENTS

Introduction: The Story So Far

Written by J.K. Rowling for the big screen, the first Fantastic Beasts movie expanded on the Wizarding World of Rowling's Harry Potter book series to tell of the adventures of Magizoologist Newt Scamander in 1926 in New York City. Now Newt's journey continues in *Fantastic Beasts: The Crimes of Grindelwald*.

As the first film begins, the world is experiencing attacks by the Dark wizard Gellert Grindelwald, who is trying to seize power over the entire wizarding community. Newt Scamander arrives in New York City with a case full of magical creatures he has rescued or is nursing back to health with the hope that a book he is writing will educate the wizarding public to the value of these remarkable beasts. He also has the goal of releasing a Thunderbird named Frank back

into his native environment in Arizona. But when he bumps into the No-Maj (or "non-magical") Jacob Kowalski, they accidentally switch cases, and Jacob unknowingly frees several of Newt's creatures into the city.

At the same time that Newt and Jacob are searching for the escaped creatures, a very dangerous magical force is destroying buildings and streets in the city. Investigating this unexplainable terror is Tina Goldstein, a former Auror at the Magical Congress of the United States of America (MACUSA). Simultaneously, Mary Lou Barebone, head of the New Salem Philanthropic Society, along with her adopted son, Credence, and adopted daughters, Chastity and Modesty, is trying to convince New Yorkers that witches exist and are causing this destruction.

Newt, Jacob, Tina, and her sister, Queenie, join forces to recover the beasts, as MACUSA now suspects the creatures are causing the damage. When Tina brings Newt into MACUSA, he meets Percival Graves, the Director of Magical Security, and tries to explain that his creatures are not responsible. But Graves discovers a different type of beast in Newt's case: an Obscurus, a Dark force that evolves from a magical child who is not allowed to develop his or her powers. Newt had separated this Obscurus from its host child, known as an Obscurial, so it is now unable to manifest any power, but Graves becomes fascinated with its possibilities.

As the events of *Fantastic Beasts and Where to Find Them* conclude, the Dark energy let loose in the city is discovered to be another Obscurus, and even worse, the Obscurial is Credence Barebone, whom Tina had been trying to rescue from his abusive adoptive mother. Newt and Tina do their best to help him, until MACUSA's Aurors seem to destroy the Obscurus. Then Percival Graves is discovered to be a Transfigured Gellert Grindelwald, whom MACUSA apprehends.

Fortunately, Newt is able to employ Frank the Thunderbird to Obliviate the memories of the No-Majs in New York who have witnessed the destruction caused by the Obscurus and the magical measures taken to stop it. Newt has Frank release a vial of Swooping Evil venom into rain clouds that soak the city and watches as he flies away. Sadly, the venom also removes the memories of Jacob Kowalski, who has formed a romantic relationship with Queenie and a deep friendship with Newt. When we last see Newt Scamander, he is leaving New York City to return to London to finish his book, promising Tina that he will hand-deliver a copy to her when it's published.

Newt's next adventure, *Fantastic Beasts: The Crimes of Grindelwald*, as producer David Heyman explains it, "is about so many things. It's about the search for Grindelwald and the search of Credence for his identity. It's a love story and a thriller and a comedy. It's about yearning and longing and love and all that stands in the way of that. It's emotionally potent and it's exciting and it's magical." *Fantastic Beasts: The Crimes of Grindelwald* enriches the wizarding world as Newt, Tina, Queenie, and Jacob visit new magical places and well-visited locations during a different time period. It introduces many new characters, good and evil, and reintroduces familiar friends at crossroads in their lives. So now, the story continues. . . .

CREDENCE SURVIVES

At the conclusion of *Fantastic Beasts and Where to Find Them*, Aurors from New York's Magical Congress of the United States of America (MACUSA) attack Credence in his Obscurus form, and it seems as if they destroy him. But no one sees a small tatter of black matter float up and beyond the City Hall subway ruins, disappearing into the sky.

THE TRUTH OF THE MATTER

"You could with justice have believed that Credence had been killed at the end of the first film," says screenwriter J.K. Rowling. "But, in fact, as Newt knows, you can't kill an Obscurial when they're in their Obscurus form. You can shatter the Obscurus temporarily, but the person hasn't died. So Credence survives and his big question now is 'Who am I?'"

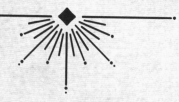

A NEW LOOK

Makeup and hair designer Fae Hammond found it exciting to visualize the changes Credence experiences as he sets out to find his real mother. "When he leaves New York, his head is shaved," she says. Her idea was that he would be harder to spot that way and would blend in with the crowd. "When he gets to Paris, he's got a short, simple crop. And the haircut is—it sounds awful—ratty. We've kept him quite tired-looking, quite dirty. But he's underground. We don't know who he is anymore."

Credence Barebone

Credence must find a way to get to Paris to search for his mother, so he joins the Circus Arcanus, which is traveling there. This magical circus features a stunning grouping of amazing creatures as well as bizarre Underbeings without powers but of magical ancestry from around the world.

GRINDELWALD ESCAPES!

Elsewhere, MACUSA prepares to transfer Gellert Grindelwald to Europe, where he will be tried for his crimes. A Thestral-drawn carriage is used as a mobile prison cell. The Thestrals take off from the Woolworth Building's attic and plummet down its side, stretching their wings to soar over the Hudson River and then to the ocean. "It's a really complex sequence," says supervising art director Martin Foley, "and it'll probably make a good roller-coaster ride in a few years!"

VALIDATED BY: D Alred
MINISTRY OFFICIAL Bo. 48524

CASE NO.
935-470/F
MACUSA-FBCERO No. 935

MAGICAL CONGRESS OF THE UNITED STATES OF AMERICA

DEPARTMENT FOR CONFISCATED ITEMS
(In accordance with MACUSA INVESTIGATION DEPARTMENT (MID) terms of conduct and by law No. 3748/274.)

→ 0935 - NY470 / F ←

NAME OF OFFENDER: GELLERT GRINDELWALD

PROHIBITED ITEMS SEIZED

A CONFISCATED ITEM: WAND
GRADES OF VIOLATION
← 1 2 3 4 5 6 7 8 (9) X →

B CONFISCATED ITEM: VIAL * UNKNOWN *
GRADES OF VIOLATION
← 1 2 3 4 5 6 7 8 9 (X) →

C CONFISCATED ITEM:
GRADES OF VIOLATION
← 1 2 3 4 5 6 7 8 9 X →

PLEASE REFER TO THE FOLLOWING LAWS:
8.36   o   2.32   ○
8.45   o   3.3   ○
24.30.10   6.37   5   ○
9.10 1   4.37   42   ○
29.6   o   930.2   ○
88.9   o   759.0   ○
83.19.11   7.36   3   Ⓧ
5.7 9   1.44   77   Ⓧ
7.24   o   2.9   ○
26.25.18   5.56   7   ○
42 21 . 37 . 17   ○
45   18.44.11   ○
38   26.25.18   Ⓧ
67.36.23 5.34 7   ○

NOTES: ***URGENT***
Suspicious vial seized.
Urgent investigation necessary to establish origin and magical capabilities.
DANGER LEVELS UNKNOWN

VALIDATED BY

CONFISCATED ITEM - LEVEL 9
(In accordance with MACUSA INVESTIGATION DEPARTMENT (MID) terms of conduct and by law No. 3748/274. Definitions of articles can be reviewed by application (by writ) to MACUSA chief of staff, stating code 84/1.)

CONFISCATED ITEM: WAND
NAME OF OFFENDER: GELLERT GRINDELWALD

CASE NO.
935-470/F
MACUSA-FBCERO No. 935

GRADES OF VIOLATION
← 1 2 3 4 5 6 7 8 (9) X →

VALIDATED BY D Alred

PRISONER EXTRADITION
(In accordance with MACUSA INVESTIGATION DEPARTMENT (MID) terms of conduct and by law No. 3748/274. Definitions of articles can be reviewed by application (by writ) to MACUSA chief of staff, stating code 84/1.)

MAGICAL CONGRESS OF THE UNITED STATES OF AMERICA
INTERNATIONAL CONFEDERATION OF WIZARDS

CRIMINAL NAME: GELLERT GRINDELWALD

STATISTICAL DETAILS:
PLEASE CLEARLY COMPLETE TO THE BEST OF YOUR ABILITY
DATE OF BIRTH: UNCONFIRMED
BIRTHPLACE: COUNTRY UNKNOWN / TOWN X / STATE:
PROFILE: EYE COLOUR Blue / HAIR COLOUR Blonde / WEIGHT 11 . 7 / HEIGHT 6 ' 3"
SCARS/MARKS: Very pale skin

REGISTERED AUTHORITY

CASE NO. MACUSA-FBCERO No. 935

UNIFORM UNIFORMS

Grindelwald and the other prisoners in the MACUSA cellblocks wear costumes that were based on Japanese firemen's uniforms. Johnny Depp (who plays Grindelwald) requested that cobwebs be added to his outfit, since his character has been sitting in his cell for almost six months.

The original Thestral puppet head from *Harry Potter and the Order of the Phoenix* was taken out of storage and used as reference for the actors and crew.

CHANGING PLACES

A deception of the highest order allows Grindelwald to escape: the prisoner MACUSA transfers isn't Grindelwald at all, but Abernathy, Tina Goldstein's Wand Permit Office supervisor, who switched places with Grindelwald at some point. So two prisoner costumes in different sizes were made for Johnny Depp and Kevin Guthrie (who plays Abernathy), and additional versions were made for their stunt doubles. Disguised as Abernathy, Grindelwald reacquires his wand, which has been stored while he was in prison.

INSIDE THE BOX

Grindelwald's wand—the Elder Wand—is supposed to be stored safely in a MACUSA lockbox. When the Auror Spielman (played by Wolf Roth) checks the box for the wand, however, he finds a nasty surprise. The wand is gone and has been replaced by a Chupacabra—a lizardlike creature with six legs, long jagged teeth, and a foul disposition.

DRY FOR WET

Grindelwald casts a spell to fill the carriage cabin with water during his escape. For this, the production crew used a process called "dry for wet," where no water is actually involved. "Wire rigs are used to get that 'floating' look," says assistant stunt coordinator Marc Mailley, "which is quite tricky to get correct." A wind machine is used to create the effect of hair moving in the water, "and the actors give slow-mo reactions, all to make it look like they're underwater."

NEWT SCAMANDER

Newt Scamander has finished his manuscript for *Fantastic Beasts and Where to Find Them*, and it's been published by Obscurus Books in London. "Newt's book has made him a bit of a celebrity," says Eddie Redmayne, "which he finds brilliantly awkward." But Newt is less concerned with his new fame than with his desire to deliver a copy of the book to Tina Goldstein as promised. "Newt's been desperately trying to get back to New York, because he wants to see Tina again," says Eddie. "But a load of bureaucracy and dodgy dealings are stopping that from happening. So when you find him at the beginning of the film, he's trying to get his travel permit to get back to New York to find Tina."

"This is a man who's happiest alone in a jungle, dealing with some fearsome creature that no other wizard would want to go near," says J.K. Rowling. "Now people want his autograph, and that's hideous for him. He thought his book was going to protect and save creatures and educate his fellow wizards, but it's made his life far more difficult."

CITIFIED

Newt's clothes have changed a bit from the coat and outfit he wore in *Fantastic Beasts and Where to Find Them.* "The silhouette and shape are very much the same," says costume designer Colleen Atwood. "I took his colors and made them more urban, more subdued, a little more grown-up, less of the creature, more of the city. But inside, he has color that you get a glimpse of every once in a while to tie him in with his beasts."

A CHANGE FOR THE BETTER

"Newt's always been his own person, and he's not good with other people, and I don't think he understands why," says Eddie Redmayne. "He's just rubbed a lot of people the wrong way by being entirely himself. But through the adventure of the first film, he found people who saw the good in him, and I think that has not only opened his heart a bit but made him walk taller, look people in the eye, and feel, perhaps, a bit more confident."

Grindelwald's growing threat to the wizarding world is at odds with Newt's longing to keep his own world confined to his creatures and his few new friends. "He doesn't want to be pulled to anyone's side," says Eddie Redmayne. "Yet because the stakes going on in the world are so high now, he's being pulled in different directions. Part of his journey now is . . . realizing that although he's always taken his own route through life, there come moments when you have to choose a side."

Newt Scamander

LONDON:
RETURN TO THE MINISTRY OF MAGIC

While at the Ministry of Magic, Newt learns he's been banned from travel because of the events with the Obscurus in New York. He finds himself being interviewed by various Ministry officials—including Torquil Travers, Head of Magical Law Enforcement, and Newt's own brother, Theseus Scamander—who are trying to convince him to help capture and destroy the Obscurus. Upon learning that Credence is still alive, Newt refuses to help them.

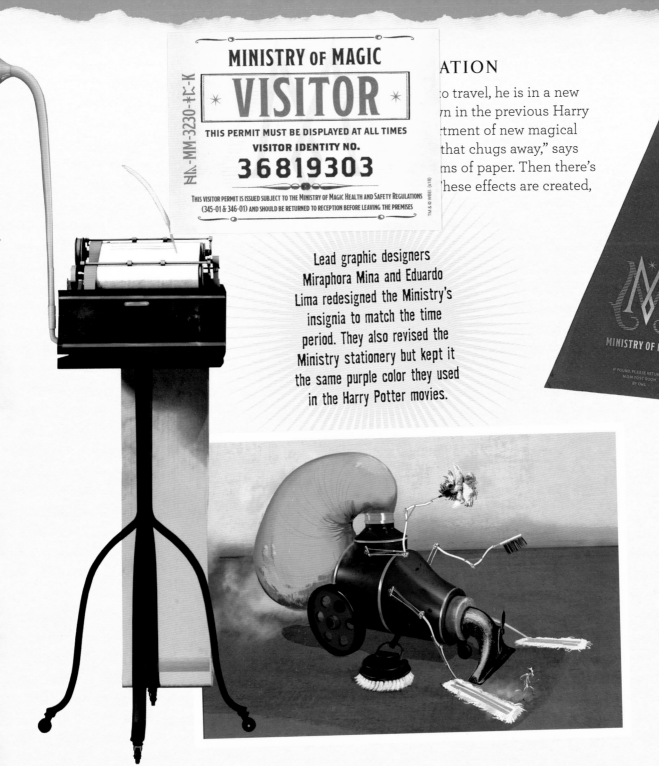

MINISTRY OF MAGIC
★ VISITOR ★
THIS PERMIT MUST BE DISPLAYED AT ALL TIMES
VISITOR IDENTITY NO.
36819303
THIS VISITOR PERMIT IS ISSUED SUBJECT TO THE MINISTRY OF MAGIC HEALTH AND SAFETY REGULATIONS (345-01 & 346-01) AND SHOULD BE RETURNED TO RECEPTION BEFORE LEAVING THE PREMISES

...ATION

...to travel, he is in a new
...wn in the previous Harry
...rtment of new magical
...that chugs away," says
...ms of paper. Then there's
...hese effects are created,

Lead graphic designers Miraphora Mina and Eduardo Lima redesigned the Ministry's insignia to match the time period. They also revised the Ministry stationery but kept it the same purple color they used in the Harry Potter movies.

MINISTRY OF MAGIC

IF FOUND, PLEASE RETURN TO
M.O.M POST ROOM
BY OWL

DUSTUP

Down the corridors of the Ministry chugs a machine that dusts the walls and floors. For *Harry Potter and the Order of the Phoenix*, a Ministry sweeper was conceived, but not realized, by concept artist Adam Brockbank. For this new film, concept artist Molly Sole was asked if she could create one for the 1927 Ministry. "It was [set decorator] Anna Pinnock's idea that it's leaving as much dust behind as it's actually cleaning up," says Molly. "There's a great big bag on the back losing dust left, right, and center." And as it goes along, "if you're too close to it, it will dust you," says prop modeler Pierre Bohanna.

THESEUS SCAMANDER

Theseus Scamander, played by Callum Turner, is Newt's older brother and Head of the Auror Office at the Ministry of Magic. Callum and Eddie found it easy to play brothers after they discovered they had grown up near each other. "He's from Chelsea and I'm from Chelsea," says Callum. "We grew up about ten minutes away from each other and probably passed each other a thousand times. If you're from a certain part of the world, there's a similar energy." Although Callum plays Newt's older brother, he's actually nine years younger than Eddie.

SPOT-ON

Hair and makeup designer Fae Hammond didn't have to do much with Callum Turner's hair in order to make it look like he and Eddie Redmayne were brothers, just lighten it. Her challenge, however, was that Callum has no freckles, and Eddie has a well-known smattering across his face. "So one of my team . . . carefully freckled him up," says Fae. "But it's a work of art and really necessary," she confirms. Freckling took about fifty minutes each day.

THE ENVELOPE, PLEASE

Callum Turner has been a fan of the Wizarding World since his childhood.
"When I was about ten, my mom bought me the first book," he remembers.
"I wasn't much of a reader, but I just blasted through it. And most nights
I went to bed hoping that Hedwig would drop a letter in my house saying
I'm going to Hogwarts." Although his letter never came, Callum is absolutely
thrilled that he gets to play a character who went to the wizarding school.

BROTHERLY LOVE

Theseus is very high up in the Ministry of Magic, "so that's how he decides
to fight the good fight," says Callum Turner. "Whereas Newt is part of the
rebellion—that's how I look at it—and Theseus is part of the establishment.
They're actually on the same side but just fighting in a different way." But
no matter what, "they're brothers. They love each other."

Leta Lestrange

Leta Lestrange comes from a rich, pure-blood wizarding family and works at the Ministry of Magic. Actress Zoë Kravitz, who plays Leta, knew a bit about Leta's family, as a descendant of hers—Bellatrix Lestrange—plays a villainous role in the story of Harry Potter. "I also knew that there was some history between Leta and Newt. And that's all I knew," says Zoë.

WOULD-BE WITCH

Zoë Kravitz admits that she has been into magic from a young age. "I would buy books and try to do spells. I think witches and the whole world of magic [are] fascinating, and it's something that I still believe exists." Acting in *Fantastic Beasts: The Crimes of Grindelwald* fulfilled her ultimate childhood fantasy.

LIGHT AND SHADOW

"When we meet her," says J.K. Rowling, "we feel that she's a woman who's struggling to emerge into the light, but she's burdened by her past. Her family casts this enormous shadow over her. At this point in wizarding history, the Lestranges are the very epitome of pure-blood aristocracy."

THE CHERRY ON TOP

"Leta Lestrange is a beautiful aristocrat [to] the manor born," says costume designer Colleen Atwood. "She wears elegant, glamorous clothes for the period, and Zoë Kravitz can wear anything. So for me, and for this particular era, she's the perfect person to dress." One of Colleen's favorite costumes for Leta was a deep Bing cherry color. "It's a moody, dark color, but it is color!"

LETA'S SECRET

"Leta has a secret that unravels during the course of this film," says Zoë, "and it's always very interesting to investigate guilt. She was explained to me as a woman who isn't quite sure where she fits in terms of being good or bad. I think she's somewhere in-between."

A COUPLE IN LOVE

Leta Lestrange, whose picture we saw in Newt's shed in *Fantastic Beasts and Were to Find Them*, is engaged to Newt's brother, Theseus. "The relationship between Theseus and Leta is they're in love with each other," says Callum Turner. "They may argue, but ultimately, they know that they're good for each other and they want to be with each other and fight the good fight together."

ALBUS DUMBLEDORE IN LONDON

Newt Scamander has a secret meeting with his former teacher, Albus Dumbledore, that moves from the dome of St. Paul's Cathedral to London's backstreets, the Victoria Bus Station, and finally Lambeth Bridge to escape being followed. Dumbledore is, of course, much younger than the familiar headmaster of Hogwarts who guided Harry Potter. "We discover that Dumbledore was partly responsible for Newt going to New York City," says producer David Heyman. "And he is ultimately responsible for Newt going to Paris."

BECOMING DUMBLEDORE

Initially, Jude Law wasn't going to watch the performances of Richard Harris or Michael Gambon, who portrayed Dumbledore in the Harry Potter films. "But I couldn't resist," he says. "First, it was an opportunity to watch the films again, which was fun, but I also wanted to see if there was anything I could get from their performances, even though it was very important to all of us that we weren't creating *that* Dumbledore. We were creating a man who was going to *become* that Dumbledore."

NICOLAS FLAMEL
51 Rue de Montmorency
Paris

erns about
ells him the
hat a rumor
rother might
jects might
gloved hand
in case he

HAND IN GLOVE

Newt and Dumbledore first meet on the dome of St. Paul's after the older wizard's floating glove beckons Newt to join him at the top of the three-hundred-year-old building. Eddie loved the way Dumbledore made his entrance. "It's just so . . . Dumbledore!"

THE BEARD

Men in the 1920s rarely sported beards. "The beard makes him stand out, and I love it," says Jude. "It makes him somewhat unusual in this time period, and I loved the idea that he was this slightly flamboyant but professorial bookworm."

—————◇—————

CLOTHES MAKE THE WIZARD

"Dumbledore in the Harry Potter films wears plummy colors, which is fine for a robe but didn't seem right for real clothes," says Colleen Atwood, so she chose heathery green-grays. "Dumbledore is somewhat a part of an underground movement in the wizarding world," says Jude Law, "and his coat gives him a certain hint of a spy."

NEWT'S BASEMENT MENAGERIE

One of the most amazing locations in *Fantastic Beasts and Where to Find Them* is the interior of Newt's case, which is composed of endless magical environments for the beasts he travels with or rescues during his adventures. For *Fantastic Beasts: The Crimes of Grindelwald*, production designer Stuart Craig created an entire basement in which to make his own magic.

AT HOME

"Newt lives in this pretty stark, slightly dry 'show' apartment in South London," says Eddie Redmayne. "But Newt being Newt, you go down into the basement and you find this absolutely mind-boggling menagerie, a hospital where he's looking after these injured and damaged creatures. Upstairs is not really where his world is. It's only when you go down into the menagerie that you see Newt's character and personality in his real life," he explains. "That's where his home is."

SLEEPING HABITATS

One question that came up was whether Newt sleeps in his apartment. "And that didn't make sense to me," says Eddie. "He's a man that's much more at home traveling through the jungle or out in the field. He had lived in his case for the year that he was collecting the information for *Fantastic Beasts*." Eddie felt that Newt would live down in the basement, probably sleeping in a hammock.

The stairs in Newt's basement give a nod to the moving staircases at Hogwarts.

DOWN IN THE BASEMENT

Newt has applied some magic to the basement of his Georgian townhouse and set up environments for his creatures in the brick archways within its walls. "And with the help of visual effects, there are landscapes and habitats for the creatures that go on and on," says Stuart Craig. "There's some complicated magic going on there." The stairs in Newt's menagerie act like supporting cantilevers in the room, which couldn't be achieved without filmic magic.

BUNTY

Victoria Yeates plays Bunty, Newt's assistant. "They have a wonderful friendship, and Newt cares for Bunty," Eddie Redmayne explains. "She has a bit of a soft spot, or quite a *strong* soft spot for him. But Newt, of course, is completely oblivious to it." Supervising art director Martin Foley was relieved when he heard about Bunty, "because you obviously worry about who's looking after all the creatures when he's off on his adventures!"

IN JUSTICE

J.K. Rowling thinks that people with modern sensibilities will view Newt's approach to these creatures as entirely ordinary. "But the world hasn't always been like that," she explains, "and actually in some parts of the world right now, obviously that is not the view that people take of the natural world. So that's at the core of Newt as a character. He's actually defying the wizarding law of the time to save some of these creatures."

SHEDDING LIGHT ON A . . . SHED

At first, Newt's basement just consisted of the many levels of staircases, his work area, and the beasts' environments. "Then Stuart decided to put Newt's tall, thin shed in the middle, which was inside his case in the first film," says Martin Foley. "I remember David Heyman asking, 'How can it be there? It's in his case. His case is on the table. How can the shed be here?'" As they tried to work out the logic of it, Stuart simply said, "You're cutting through all these crossing staircases. It looks amazing."

Old Friends

When asked which is his favorite beast, Eddie Redmayne is reluctant to choose just one, but more often than not, he admits that it's Pickett the Bowtruckle. "Newt has a soft spot for him," says Eddie. "*I* have a soft spot for him. He's just so small and twiglike and sweet."

THE ULTIMATE TREE HOUSE

Pickett has a habitat in Newt's basement and another on Newt's workspace. "There's a tree on his desk," says Pierre Bohanna, "so Pickett can jump out of his pocket and just go for a little snooze, a little rest. Take it easy, chew a leaf."

Robin Guiver describes Pickett's rod maneuvers as like operating three chopsticks with one hand.

THE PICK(ETT) OF THE BUNCH

Although he's rather small, Pickett is a big responsibility for puppeteer Robin Guiver. "He's actually the most technically complicated puppet we have to work with," Robin explains. "We use long rods that are very spindly. He's tiny, as well. But I've really grown to love our Pickett puppet. We can really express a lot in the relationship between Newt and Pickett. And so, every time we get to a scene where he's there, it's really enjoyable to work out what his action will be and how he's involved."

NIFFLER

"The Niffler's back with a vengeance!" proclaims Eddie Redmayne. The actor was excited the Niffler had returned, and now there are even more Nifflers. "The Nifflers had babies. So there's not only one scene-stealer, there's now an entire family of scene-stealers. They're causing Newt quite a headache," Eddie says, "but trying to wrangle a fleet of little babies was one of my most enjoyable scenes."

"The Niffler is absolutely everyone's favorite," says puppeteer Robin Guiver. "He's small and cuddly and intelligent and cheeky, and in both the last film and this one, has a big impact on the story."

A TREASURE TROVE OF NIFFLERS

For our baby Nifflers, "we have ones that have a little rod in their heads and are really good at looking and interacting and making eye contact," says puppeteer Robin Guiver. "We've got ones that are on the end of sticks that we can run around very fast. We've got ones that are just like a big, black, weighted beanbag." All these different versions help the actors figure out their physical interactions with the creatures and give a sense of their feel and weight.

NEW BEASTS

The Kelpie that Newt has rescued is an underwater creature with equine features and long seaweed-like tendrils. Kelpies are extremely strong and hard to tame, and have a nasty bite. But for those who know how to handle it, the Kelpie can provide a fast underwater ride. The animators studied horses, jellyfish, and squid for their movements. In *The Crimes of Grindelwald*, Newt goes into the Kelpie's underwater environment to apply ointment to a wound and ends up taking a wild ride.

DEEP DIVE

The scene with Newt riding the Kelpie was shot in one of the biggest underwater filming tanks in Europe, and Eddie Redmayne was asked to do the bulk of the stunt himself. Eddie learned how to work with scuba-diving gear and perform the proper breath-holds. The stunt had him dragged through the water on a rig, breaking the surface, and riding out. "And Eddie absolutely smashed it!" says assistant stunt coordinator Marc Mailley.

LEUCROTTA

The Leucrotta resembles a stag or moose but has an enormous mouth. *Enormous!* "We needed Bunty to put her head into the Leucrotta's mouth and look around," says Robin Guiver. "We used a big iron hoop, which didn't really do anything, but we put eyes on top of it and a big bag below, so it gave the right shadows and gave Victoria [Yeates, who plays Bunty] something to interact with."

AUGUREY

When Jacob explores the menagerie, he meets the Augurey, an owl-like bird that Newt is caring for. The Augurey joins Jacob as he wanders around the area. "So we mocked up a little puppet," says Robin, "who followed him around." When the Augurey flew, the puppeteers used a foam football with sprayed-on eyes and some simple feathers for the actors to focus on.

HINKYPUNK

Newt takes a Hinkypunk, a wisplike creature, with him to Paris. Hinkypunks can be helpful because they disrupt tracking charms.

TAKING CARE OF THE BEASTS

Newt's basement contains loads of equipment and supplies to help cure any ills his beasts may develop. Medicines include a line of creams that provide pain relief for all types of creatures and dried Billywig stings, which Newt used to cure Jacob's Murtlap bite in the first Fantastic Beasts film. Food supplies include spiders, moths, woodlice, and mushrooms.

Newt uses a special eye dropper to treat the enormous eyes of one of his Mooncalves.

A MAGIZOOLOGIST'S EQUIPMENT

Set decorator Anna Pinnock went to ZSL London Zoo and checked out their veterinary department. There, she saw "bits of string and pipe and cardboard—things vets use to improvise medical equipment for animals. We tried to do much the same thing." There's also a huge X-ray machine for Newt's use. "That was based on a 1950s X-ray machine," says Anna. "We also had a great big operating light based on one from the same time period, but we added things to it. That's what's so much fun, actually—adding one era's details into something from a different era."

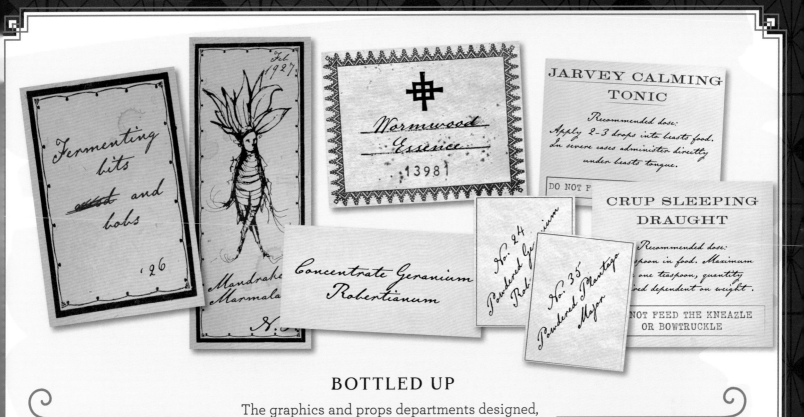

Labels shown:
- Fermenting bits and bobs '26
- Feb. 1927 · Mandrake Marmala...
- Wormwood Essence 13981
- JARVEY CALMING TONIC — Recommended dose: Apply 2–3 drops into beasts food. In severe cases administer directly under beasts tongue.
- DO NOT F...
- Concentrate Geranium Robertianum
- No. 24 Powdered Ge...
- No. 35 Powdered Plantago Major
- CRUP SLEEPING DRAUGHT — Recommended dose: ...spoon in food. Maximum ...one teaspoon, quantity ...ired dependent on weight. ...NOT FEED THE KNEAZLE OR BOWTRUCKLE

BOTTLED UP

The graphics and props departments designed, hand-lettered, and applied elixir, potion, and tincture labels to bottles of all sizes.

ALL IN A DAY'S WORK

"Working with beasts that will be computer generated is hilarious," says Eddie Redmayne. "It's as weird and odd as you'd imagine it to be. Sometimes you're working with nothing. Pickett, for example, you just imagine him there. Sometimes you're looking at a mark on a stick. Other times you have these amazing puppeteers doing extraordinary things. Occasionally you have men in full-body morph green suits looking ridiculous, and you're trying to pretend that they're some wondrous fantastical creature. It makes you go home every night feeling really tired because your imagination has been squished from every side. But I love it!"

Queenie Goldstein

The romance between the witch Queenie Goldstein and the No-Maj Jacob Kowalski is forbidden in the wizarding world of New York and seemed to have ended when Jacob was Obliviated at the end of *Fantastic Beasts and Where to Find Them*. Now, many months later, we learn that Queenie has helped Jacob get his memories back of their time together and taken him with her to London.

PLAID FAD

When Alison Sudol learned her character was going to England, she "just felt that Queenie would want to coordinate with her surroundings." Alison requested that Colleen Atwood make her an outfit out of tartan, which she did using a real plaid fabric from the thirties. Colleen also gave Queenie a tweed coat and more jewelry to wear than before. "Queenie's still incredibly feminine," says Colleen, "but she's more grown-up and sophisticated."

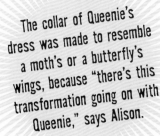

The collar of Queenie's dress was made to resemble a moth's or a butterfly's wings, because "there's this transformation going on with Queenie," says Alison.

THE HEART RULES THE HEAD

Queenie leaves New York with Jacob because the laws about relationships with No-Majs are less strict in Europe than they are in the United States. "There are really stringent laws about what interaction you can have with No-Majs," Alison says, "which is basically 'stay out of their way.'"

WRONG AND RIGHT

"She's breaking the rules by coming back to Jacob," says Alison. "You can see that they've been in a relationship for a while, and it's caused a huge rift with her sister Tina. And Queenie's going to have Jacob whether Jacob likes it or not," she continues, "and it doesn't work out very well. That sets her off on a journey alone," where Alison feels her character "just gets really *lost*. I can see she's on a necessary path toward wisdom and maturity, but it's not going to be easy."

JACOB KOWALSKI

"Queenie is dragging Jacob along [through] the British countryside to get the gang back together," says Dan Fogler, who plays Jacob. "They find Newt, and right away Newt asks, 'What's wrong with him?' because I'm a little bit too jolly, too happy to be there." It's discovered that Queenie has put him under a spell. "That first scene was so much fun to play," Dan remembers. "I'm pouring tons of salt on my food and pouring stuff on my head—it's like I'm drunk on life."

ANOTHER PLAID FAD

Jacob has become a successful baker in New York, and his wardrobe reflects that. "His suit fits a lot better now," says Colleen Atwood. "All the pieces are from the same fabric, and his shoes are out of the same fabric to match, to give him flair." The fabric used was very fine English wool in a blue-and-black plaid. A total of eight matching suits were made: five for Dan, one for his double, and two for his stuntman.

NO MAJ, NO PROBLEM

"The beautiful thing about Jacob," says Dan, "is that he finds himself in the middle of chaos but he's such a good person that he's like, 'How did I find myself here? This is insane but, yes, I'll help you until the end of your journey.' His heart is so big that he can't help but help people." Dan says his own reaction would be, "What? Wait, what? Hold on, get me out of here! I'm not risking my life again!"

STORMY WEATHER

When Newt removes the spell Queenie has placed on Jacob, Jacob quickly realizes that Queenie had enchanted him to get him out of New York, which makes him upset. They quarrel and Queenie leaves, running out into the rain. Dan feels that even though the story is about a magical society, "it has its roots in real relationships, and that's why it's so relatable."

TINA GOLDSTEIN

Actress Katherine Waterston feels that when Tina was demoted from being an Auror, "she was nervous about her career, but she never fully lost her confidence. She was following her instincts in the first film, and that led to Grindelwald's arrest." Now Tina is applying those instincts as she tries to find and save Credence.

TINA AND CREDENCE

Katherine thinks the reason Tina is drawn to Credence is because of her feelings for her own sister. "Tina felt a great responsibility to protect Queenie when they were orphaned," Katherine explains, "and that expanded to protect any child. I think that's what initially drew her to Credence." Tina gave him her word that she and Newt would protect him. "And Tina's not one to go back on her word."

ENCHANTED DISPATCHES TO THE AM

THE NEW YOR

VOL. LXVII NO. 221254A- DAILY

THURSDAY 6TH JANUARY 1927

EXCLUSIVE ★ EXCLUSIVE FEARLESS

PORPENTINA GOLDSTEIN (RE)APPOINTED AS AUROR

MACUSA HEADQUARTERS – NYC.

President Picquery to award Ms. Goldstein

Presidential affairs

SPECIAL REPORT
IS THE WIZARDING COMMUNITY NOW AT PEACE?
by E.L. Filtrie

GRIN EXTR DATE C

MACUSA HEADQUARTERS – NYC.

OTHER NEWS
Alaska wartock

Makeup and hair designer Fae Hammond feels that Tina's new haircut shows she's really in control. "You can't beat a simple bob," says Fae, "and it makes her look very chic."

TRUE BLUE

Katherine Waterston and Colleen Atwood discussed whether Tina should wear a standard issue Auror coat. "Tina isn't confident that MACUSA would approve of her desire to save Credence," says Katherine. "She's doing this investigation on the sly." Colleen switched up the coat, giving Tina a blue leather, detective-style coat with a cinched waist. "And, man, that coat weighs so much!" says Katherine. "It's a workout just to put it on every day."

TINA AND NEWT

Tina and Newt were corresponding with each other, but she cuts communication off abruptly when she reads in a tabloid magazine that Newt is engaged to Leta Lestrange. "So she decides to get on with her life," says Katherine. "Then Newt shows up in Paris and chases her until she's forced to listen to the truth." Is there a chance for them? "There's a chance she might kick him in the shins!" she says with a laugh. "She's mad. She thinks she's been jilted. She's got her pride, so she's trying to cover it up, but, of course, he can see through that."

SENSATIONAL INCANTATIONS FOR YOUR DELECTATION! ★★★★★

WIZARD

ENQUIRER

EXCLUSIVE STORY

'CREATURE TEACHER'

NEWT TO TIE THE KNOT

BACHELOR NO MORE? MAVERICK MAGIZOOLOGIST IS ENGAGED TO WIZARDING NOBILITY! STORY ON PAGE 4

★ NEXT WEEK ★ I ACCIO'D MY OWN FEET! LATEST CROCODILE BILE CAN MAKE YOU FAT! STORY ON PAGE 3

NEWSPAPERS, BOOKS, AND MAGAZINES

For *Fantastic Beasts: The Crimes of Grindelwald*, the graphics department was tasked with creating a French wizarding newspaper, tabloid magazines, and the first editions of Newt Scamander's book, *Fantastic Beasts and Where to Find Them.*

LE CRI DE LA GARGOUILLE

The French wizarding newspaper is named *Le Cri de la Gargouille* (in English, *The Cry of the Gargoyle*). "From afar, it looks like a Muggle newspaper from the time period," says Eduardo Lima. "But the content is relevant to what's going on in the wizarding world or to the time or place," adds Miraphora Mina. Headlines on the front page echo those in the *New York Ghost*: DARK SORCERERS ARE AMONG US and FRENCH SORCERERS ARE TERRORIZED. Other articles are somewhat less frightening: 3,000 COINS ARE FOUND ON A NIFFLER IN CANNES, 297 WANDS ARE STOLEN FROM THE SHOP OF WANDMAKER COSME ACAJOR, and a reminder that the ARC DE TRIOMPHE IS NOT A PORTKEY.

TABLOID MAGS

Spellbound: Celebrity Secrets & Spell Tips of the Stars and *Wizard Enquirer: Sensational Incantations for Your Delectation* resemble the gossipy "rag" magazines of the No-Maj world. These magazines make Tina think that Newt is engaged to Leta Lestrange. One issue of *Spellbound* features a cover article about someone with a familiar last name: Fleamont Potter.

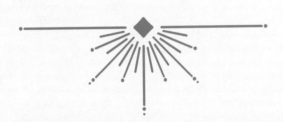

FANTASTIC BEASTS AND WHERE TO FIND THEM

Miraphora Mina and Eduardo Lima had already created an on-screen version of the textbook *Fantastic Beasts and Where to Find Them* for *Harry Potter and the Sorcerer's Stone*. This edition of Newt's book was newly published in 1927, so the design reflects the sleek modern lettering of the Art Deco style.

PARIS 1927

"Paris of the 1920s was a real melting pot of ideas creatively, artistically, and socially," says director David Yates. "It was a very vibrant time. It's a really wonderful and magnificent place to choose for this story."

Says writer J.K. Rowling, "One of the great glories and joys of the Beasts series is how free I am to go different places within the magical world, to explore different countries and every aspect of the wizarding world."

VIVE LA DIFFÉRENCE!

"Paris is very different from New York," says executive producer Tim Lewis. "It's a different culture, a different *everything*, even to the basic design of the city. New York is very symmetrical, Paris is not." And just as there wasn't enough of the real 1926 New York in New York to film, there's not a lot of 1927 Paris in 2017 Paris, so the cityscape was constructed at Leavesden Studios in the UK.

KNOWING ALL THE ANGLES

The Paris set was placed "over" the original New York set from the first film. However, "New York is a grid, but Paris is not," says Martin Foley. "It has lovely intersections with five streets all combining to one and crossing one another at great angles. So Stuart [Craig] took the New York grid and added a couple of really distinct slices. We also added elevations with steps and slopes." They left some of the first film's facades and just built in front of them. If this becomes standard practice, "[b]y the fifth film, there'll be five sets of facades in front of each other. By the last film, there will be really narrow streets!" he jokes.

Newt and Jacob take an illegal Portkey, which is in the form of a bucket, from the white cliffs of Dover to Paris.

"Everyone pretty much wore a hat in this period," says Colleen Atwood. "I've done hats that have a fantastical feeling. But it's Paris, so I can get away with it."

FRENCH FLAIR

Colleen Atwood was excited about the story being set in Paris, which has always been known for its elegance and style. For 1920s Parisian costumes, Colleen worked with a more extreme silhouette for the clothes—squarer shoulders and longer, flowing skirts. "And as the story goes into sort of a film noir vibe, it's definitely got an edgier and more dramatic style to it," she says.

GRINDELWALD IN PARIS

When Gellert Grindelwald arrives in Paris, he takes over a Non-Magique's townhouse. "Grindelwald has his agenda," says producer David Heyman. "He is trying to build support and engineer events for what he views as the 'greater good.' He believes that the wizarding world should no longer have to live in secret, that it should emerge and be the dominating force in the world."

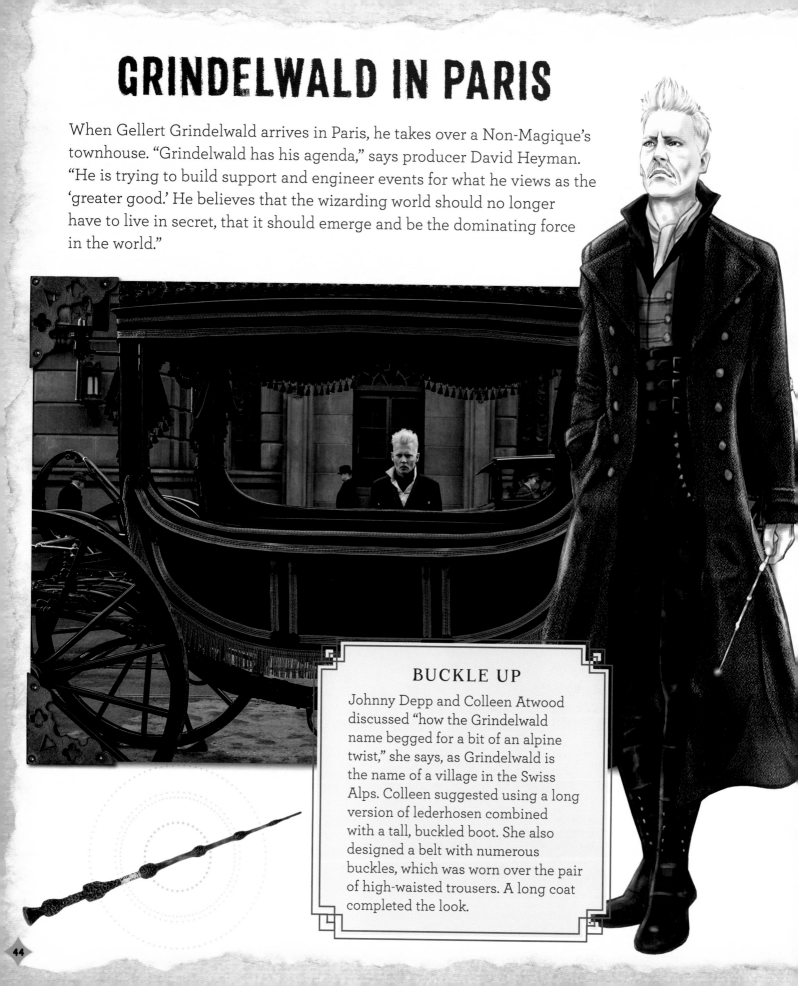

BUCKLE UP

Johnny Depp and Colleen Atwood discussed "how the Grindelwald name begged for a bit of an alpine twist," she says, as Grindelwald is the name of a village in the Swiss Alps. Colleen suggested using a long version of lederhosen combined with a tall, buckled boot. She also designed a belt with numerous buckles, which was worn over the pair of high-waisted trousers. A long coat completed the look.

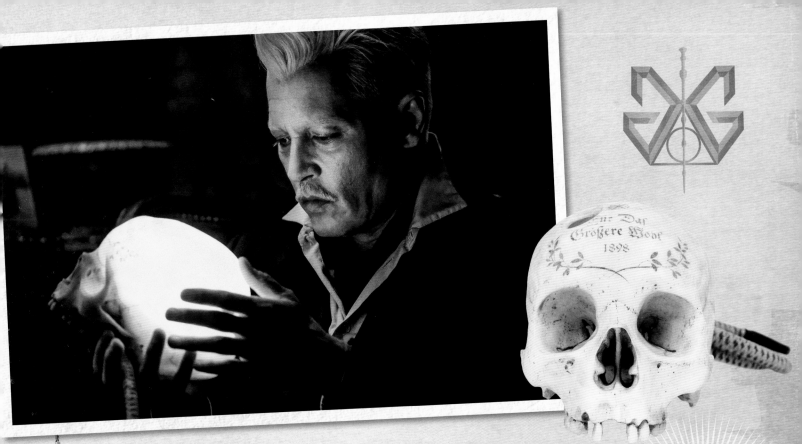

OUT OF HIS SKULL

Grindelwald extracts the thoughts and feelings of his victims and transfers them through a skull attached to a hookah pipe. The smoke he exhales while smoking this mixture produces his visions. Stuart Craig found a skull for the hookah pipe as a reference, and then visual artist Rob Bliss decorated it. "There's a history of decorating skulls in Europe," Rob explains, "and one way to commemorate the person was to paint on roses and words or names in Gothic lettering."

Für Das Größere Wohl translates as "For the greater good."

A VILE VIAL

The decoration on a vial Grindelwald wears around his neck was designed by concept artist Molly Sole. "I was thinking about what was really important to him," she explains. "He was obsessed with the Deathly Hallows, so I thought if I was designing a piece of jewelry that was personal to him, I would symbolize that."

GRINDELWALD'S ACOLYTES

Grindelwald gathers together a group of followers, and the ones who are his closest assistants are called *acolytes*. "They're a quirky group," says costume designer Colleen Atwood. For uniformity, the acolytes were dressed in jackets with multiple belts and sharp-edged hats. "But they're very different types," says Colleen. She thinks "some are planners and some are enforcers. So I tried to give each of them a detail of individuality."

VINDA ROSIER

Poppy Corby-Tuech plays Vinda Rosier, whose last name will be familiar to Harry Potter fans as it also belonged to one of Voldemort's Death Eaters. Rosier brings Queenie to Grindelwald, who lures her into his fold. "Grindelwald toes that line of being charming and terrifying really, really well," says Poppy. "He's very charismatic, and you can understand why so many people follow him, because he's very persuasive."

ABERNATHY

In *Fantastic Beasts and Where to Find Them*, Abernathy (portrayed by Kevin Guthrie) was described in the script as a "jobsworth." Guthrie now calls him "'the convert,' because he's been taken over by Grindelwald. He's a disciple for the cause, although he's more of a whipping boy." Kevin feels that Abernathy is desperate to please Grindelwald, "and I think he's prepared to go to any lengths to achieve that."

NAGEL

Nagel is played by Claudius Peters, who calls Grindelwald's followers "revolutionaries. They want to make the world a better place, from their point of view, anyway, so they're part of Grindelwald's team in order to do that." Colleen Atwood describes Claudius's face as "one that could tell a thousand stories. I felt as though he had a heavy presence without doing anything, so I kept him very thin, not heavily clothed, and elegant in his own way."

CARROW

Referred to by her last name only, Grindelwald's acolyte Carrow should also strike a chord with fans of Harry Potter. Her surname suggests she is a relative of Death Eaters Amycus and Alecto Carrow.

THE PURSUERS

YUSUF KAMA

Actor William Nadylam plays Yusuf Kama, who meets Tina at Circus Arcanus and tells her that he believes he is related to Credence. He says they are the last males of a pure-blood wizard line, but this is a lie. Yusuf imprisons Tina, and she learns that Kama wants the Obscurial dead.

"Kama was someone who came from a higher level of wizardry but had fallen on harder times," says Colleen Atwood. She was advised by director David Yates to "make him look like he's had the best clothes in the world—and he's still wearing them twenty years later."

A BREAKABLE VOW?

Yusuf Kama is another character in the story who exists between good and evil. He pursues a vengeful path due to a vow he made to his father, but when he meets Tina and later Newt, "it changes his trajectory in a way he didn't expect," says William Nadylam. "He will find out that things are not exactly what he thinks they are. He'll find goodness within himself thanks to their intervention."

Newt and Jacob find and rescue Tina, but Newt discovers that Kama suffers from water dragon parasites and treats his illness when all four characters Apparate to the safe house recommended by Dumbledore.

GUNNAR GRIMMSON

After Newt refuses to find Credence at the behest of the Ministry of Magic so they can destroy the Obscurial, the Ministry of Magic hires Gunnar Grimmson, a beast bounty hunter, to do the job. "Grimmson is like a dark twin of Newt," says David Yates. "Newt captures beasts to protect them, and Grimmson tracks them to kill them." Actor Ingvar Sigurðsson plays Grimmson, who pursued and destroyed an Obscurial fifteen years earlier.

OPPOSITE SIDES

"Grimmson is Newt's nemesis," says Eddie Redmayne. "They've clearly met before." "And they hate each other," adds Ingvar. Newt and Grimmson have totally opposite views about magical creatures. "Grimmson will kill creatures that could give away the existence of wizards," Eddie explains, "whereas Newt would be about helping them and finding a way for us to understand them to better protect them and ourselves."

PLACE CACHÉE

As we know, Hogwarts students as well as adult witches and wizards buy their robes, Quidditch equipment, and supplies for potions at Diagon Alley in London. Paris has a similar street that features wizarding shops and restaurants: Place Cachée. But this "place" has one significant difference from Diagon Alley: it's two locations in one.

The Circus Arcanus has set up on Place Cachée.

...CE
...o be just
...es. But
...d, just
...houses
No-Maj businesses as well as MACUSA.
At the top of some steps is the statue of a robed woman. If you're magical, you can pass under her through the plinth into the wizarding world. "It's a bit like entering platform nine and three-quarters," says production designer Stuart Craig.

SHOPKEEPING

Stuart Craig felt it was important to pay homage to Diagon Alley in this new movie. "In Diagon Alley, you've got the cauldron shop," says set decorator Anna Pinnock, "so we did a French version called Chaudrons with all the copper, such as the jelly molds." There's also a sweet shop—the Enchanted Confiserie—"because I just felt since there was one in Diagon Alley, it would be rude not to!"

SHOPPING SPREE

Although none of the main characters actually enters the shops at Place Cachée, it's obvious that the stores are filled to the ceiling with merchandise. Anna Pinnock and her crew shopped in numerous French flea markets and fairs in order to acquire the items. "We took trucks," says Anna, "and just bought and bought before we even had a script. And we've used *everything*." Anna also went online to find the more unique items. "The crystal balls were bought on the Internet," she says. "There was a lot of stock from the first *Fantastic Beasts* film and stock from the Potter films. There's a wealth of stuff in storage, but there's never enough, is there?"

DESIGN DELIGHT

Place Cachée offers Quidditch
equipment at Gaston McAaron,
as well as cauldrons and owls
and owl cages. "And it's quite
fun to see an earlier version
of those," says Stuart Craig. In
1927, the art movement was in a
time of change. "It wasn't quite
fully Art Deco," says Stuart,
"but modernism was there."

A WORLD OF WONDER

For *Fantastic Beasts: The Crimes of Grindelwald*, J.K. Rowling's script shows that the magical
and non-magical worlds exist simultaneously in the same locations. "One of the things that
always intoxicated me so much about J.K. Rowling's world," says Eddie Redmayne, "was we
all live our lives in our cities, but the idea that you can peel something back and there is a
more vibrant, magical, brilliant world beneath is exciting. And Paris is the perfect tapestry for
Jo [Rowling] to really start gently unfolding and showing this other world full of whimsy and
extraordinary things. I love that."

DOUBLE DUTY

Because Place Cachée is seen in both its magical and non-magical versions, the graphics and props departments needed to dress it twice. "And we had to do the same number of signs and objects for both the Non-Magique and wizarding shops. Sometimes it's quite overwhelming . . . the amount of stuff that needs to be created!" says Eduardo Lima. "And we don't really know what will get seen, so it's important to do it 100 percent," adds Miraphora Mina. One of the graphic artists' hardest challenges with dressing the sets was making everything look new. "It's an instinct for both the filmmakers and audience to want to make something from an older period look aged," says Miraphora. "But if it's a newspaper for that day, then it's new, it's fresh."

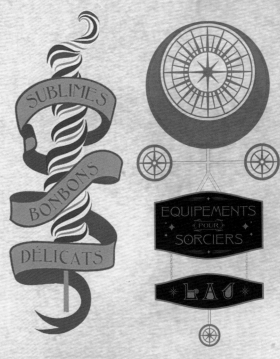

Circus Arcanus

Tina finally discovers Credence in Paris at Circus Arcanus. Although production designer Stuart Craig found the challenge of creating a magical circus very interesting, he feels that Circus Arcanus is disturbing. "We don't have clowns and clown cars, comedy cars, lions, or tigers. There are some really sad creatures in there. It's a freak show rather than a regular circus."

NOT-SO-FINE ART

Colorful banners featuring the performing beasts and acts hang in the entrance of Circus Arcanus. To mimic the style of lower-end posters printed in the 1920s, décor and lettering artist Julian Walker had to hold back from his finest work. "They're not amazingly painted," he explains, "because it would have been people back in the day who just said, 'We need this done, find an artist, any artist.' They're a bit crude, but they're full of character."

TRUE GRIT

"This circus has a grimy, gritty edge to it," says costume designer Colleen Atwood. "Everyone's costumes were made poorly. They are shredded and falling apart, with a cheap sparkle. It is a low-rent circus, and the characters all had a sadness to them. Instead of the happy circus, it feels very *noir*, beyond what anyone thinks a circus is."

◇

SKENDER

Skender runs the circus and acts as ringmaster and animal trainer. Colleen Atwood had to fashion two looks for him: a dowdy one for when he's working at the docks, and a flashy, sparkly ringmaster outfit. "He's not a very good ringmaster," says Colleen. "And he's got a dark edge to him."

INSIDE THE TENT

Circus Arcanus features Underbeings, who have magical ancestry but are without magical powers, such as half-elves and half-goblins. Inside the main tent, a half-troll performs feats of strength. Martin Foley describes the circus as "quite mean-spirited. Outside, it's all joyous and like everyone's having fun, but these Underbeings that find themselves the center of attention in there are actually a sad, moving part of the film."

Circus Arcanus advertises new exotic beasts such as the Kappa, a Japanese water demon, and the Oni, a large horned beast.

NEW BEASTS: THE ZOUWU

The Zouwu is a regal, catlike Chinese beast the size of an elephant that is capable of running one thousand miles in a day. A Zouwu is one of the magical beasts displayed at Circus Arcanus, but she's been mistreated and she's underweight and injured. During a fire that Credence starts at the circus, the Zouwu is able to escape her crate, and she disappears into the Parisian streets.

DO THE MATH

"The Zouwu can run a thousand miles in a single day," says David Yates. Mathematically, this adds up to the Zouwu's actual speed being forty-seven miles an hour, "which isn't quite that fast when you analyze it," he says with a laugh, "but it sounds wonderful."

FAST TRACKER

"When Newt first meets the Zouwu," says puppeteer Robin Guiver, "she's injured and vulnerable. And despite the fact that it's a magical beast, there's a reality to that story that we can all relate to, seeing how this happens in the real world. Newt recognizes this." The Zouwu is scared and threatens to attack Newt when he encounters her on a Parisian bridge. "Newt sees through that fear to what's going on inside it," Robin continues, "and fortunately knows how to handle her to get her into a safe place in his suitcase."

What does Newt use to tame the Zouwu? "A fluffy, furry, giant cat toy," says Christian Short. "It even squeaks a little bit and has a bell."

N.Y. 291   291-02-91-AX

BUREAU OF MAGICAL IMPORTS AND EXPORTS

MAGICAL CREATURE

CAUTION
HANDLE WITH CARE
ONLY TO BE HANDLED
BY A QUALIFIED MAGIZOOLOGIST

TEAM ZOUWU

"I think that probably some of the most enjoyable work for me on this film is getting to interact with the creatures and trying to work out the best way to do that," says Eddie Redmayne. "And it's really a team effort. It's a concoction of puppeteers, stunt specialists, movement coaches, and viz effects guys, and the Zouwu is a case in point."

THE MALEDICTUS

The Maledictus, played by Claudia Kim, is an Underbeing and the carrier of a blood curse that turns her into a snake. Eventually, the transformation will become permanent. "She's turning into a snake, but she wants to be a woman while she can," says David Yates. "So there's this really beautiful story of how she tries to cling to her humanity in the brief time that she has."

SHIFTING HEARTS

"The Maledictus is a prisoner in the circus," says Claudia Kim, "and she's also bound to become a prisoner in her own body. In this place of great hopelessness, she meets Credence, and to her, I think, Credence's desire to find out who he is, that drive, that determination, gives her hope."

SLITHERING

Visual effects brought in a real snake to be observed and cyberscanned. "The snake was beautiful," says George Bootman, a visual effects assistant coordinator. "It was about fourteen feet long, and when we took photos of it, it wasn't put off by the flashes or lights." In addition to acquiring digital references, the snake was filmed wrapped around a mannequin representing Claudia Kim so the artists could observe how the scales worked when it curled around her.

SNAKESCREEN

Colleen Atwood did not want to put the Maledictus in a snakeskin dress but did want to evoke the idea of the skin, so she found a lace material and screened a metallic foil over it. Ruffles were added around the bottom and the sleeves "to depict the coils of the snake," Colleen explains. "The dress is tango-inspired but still looks like a circus costume."

SANDS OF TIME

The relationship between Credence and the Maledictus is a really special one. "There's real love there," says Ezra Miller, "coming from two people who are both struggling in similar ways as being unusual or different, as carrying these otherworldly aspects of themselves that remove them from society. They're both hourglasses in their own right with the sand trickling away."

LE MINISTÈRE DES AFFAIRES MAGIQUES DE LA FRANCE

The French counterpart to the Ministry of Magic and MACUSA is the Ministère des Affaires Magiques. The headquarters for the Ministère was designed in the Art Nouveau style, which emphasizes organic, twisting curves. "This style was absolutely synonymous with Paris in the twenties," says Stuart Craig. "Jo [Rowling] recognized that immediately and specified it in the stage directions. So there's not much really except for little bits that we can do to surprise her!"

The entrance to the French ministry is in a square in Paris. When Queenie stands between some trees in the square, they form a birdcage-shaped elevator around her that takes her down into the main dome.

RUNNING AROUND IN CIRCLES

In previous wizarding films, government headquarters were designed conventionally, with one floor above the next, all the way to the top. "The layout we have for the French ministry is a series of interchanging, linking domes, which you go through like a tunnel," describes art director Sam Leake. The main dome is in the center, and then corridors lead to the next dome, and so on. "You can see across into the next dome [and] into the tunnel beyond. This gives it much greater depth, rather than having to look up."

LIGHT EFFECT

"Art Nouveau is all about light and nature and glass," says Martin Foley. "Each of the Ministère's domes has a glass ceiling, and they have an ethereal, magical glow, so straightaway we almost forget we're underground."

REVERT TO TYPE

Anna Pinnock was asked to create a typing pool similar to the one seen in the MACUSA basement, "because, presumably, all these institutions conform to this same format," she says. "We did find a fantastic glass-and-metal desk in a flea market in Paris, so we made the desks out of glass and metal but in a modular format that can all slot together. And then there are rows of people all doing the same thing, dressed exactly the same."

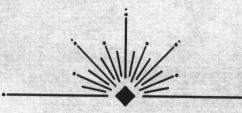

Art of the Ministère des Affaires Magiques

The French ministry features many artistic items within its domed walls, as well as a seal representing French nationalism designed in the Art Nouveau style.

OFF THE CHARTS

Projected on the ceiling of the main dome of the French ministry is a rotating celestial chart of magical beasts. "When we first did [the dome], we based it on existing astronomical charts from the eighteenth century, from beautiful engraved calendars and other items," says concept artist Dermot Power. "J.K. Rowling didn't want to use the existing zodiac chart that everybody's familiar with, so I came up with another version." Dermot pointed out to her that he didn't want to be the one to decide what *her* world's astronomical chart should be. "She said, 'I'll send you a list.'" Her list included nearly all the fantastic beasts from the first movie, plus a few more from the Harry Potter books and films. "So rather than Capricorn, it is a Graphorn," says Martin Foley.

THE BRONZE RING

Three beautiful statues encircle the balustrade that borders the main dome. They were sculpted by concept sculptor Julian Murray, who created the Magic Is Might statue for *Harry Potter and the Deathly Hallows – Part 1*. They were first made in life-size clay versions, then cyberscanned. The scan was taken to a cutting factory and carved out of high-density model-making foam—but at twice the scale, so they became twenty feet tall. Finally, they were sprayed with a finish similar to auto body paint and rubbed to a really high sheen to imitate bronze.

THE FRENCH SEAL

Miraphora Mina and Eduardo Lima designed the seal for the French ministry, which was founded in 1790, the first year after the French Revolution. "And we created all the paperwork to support the ministry," says Eduardo Lima. "Luckily, our graphics coordinator was French!"

NEW BEASTS: THE MATAGOTS

One of the new beasts we encounter in *Fantastic Beasts: The Crimes of Grindelwald* is the feline Matagot. The Matagot is a spirit familiar somewhat resembling a hairless Sphinx cat. In France, they are utlitized by the Ministère des Affaires Magiques to do menial jobs, including staffing the mailroom and providing security for various other departments. Matagots won't attack unless provoked, but then they will transform into something far more menacing. Director David Yates describes them as unusual cats: "They're very surreal, and that's why they're fantastic."

THE CAT'S MEOW

Puppeteers portrayed the Matagots to give the actors eyelines and to understand their interaction. Puppeteer Tom Wilton calls the Matagots "wonderful spiritual cat guardian creatures. Physically embodying them meant that, take after take after take, we were 'quadrupeding' on all fours, crawling along to the top deck of this beautiful set, being catlike."

ESCAPE FROM CIRCUS ARCANUS

When Tina Goldstein locates Credence at Circus Arcanus, she meets Yusuf Kama, who is also looking for Credence. Unbeknownst to both Tina and Yusuf, Credence has made plans to escape with the Maledictus that same day. "He's just cast off the chains of the abuse that he suffered through his whole youth," says Ezra Miller. "But the circus is also an abusive environment, so he intentionally breaks out because he recognizes that it's just another cage."

MAGIC UNLIKE ANY OTHER

Credence is still an Obscurial, but he has gained control of the Obscurus. "He has an awareness that he is in this relationship with the Obscurus and now is starting to gain a means to manifest the Obscurus intentionally," says Ezra. "There's a freedom and a relief to that because he was so victimized, and this transforms him into someone who's surviving."

FIRE EXIT

Credence escapes with the Maledictus by releasing firedrakes into the crowd. As the circus catches on fire, Tina tries to get to Credence but in the chaos cannot reach him.

The sparks that Firedrakes emit from their tails set anything flammable ablaze.

"Everyone's looking for Credence," says Ezra. "Everyone's hunting Credence. Various facets of the wizarding community are interested in Credence for different reasons. He is a threat to everyone."

Irma's Attic

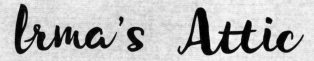

Credence and the Maledictus go to meet Irma, the
woman whose name is on his adoption papers, who
lives in a small attic space. But the occupant turns
out to be an Underbeing—half-elf, half-human. Irma is
about to give Credence important information about
his mother when Grimmson interrupts them.

WAIT AND SEE

To build anticipation and tension about Credence's arrival at the address he's been given, thinking he's about to meet his mother, he's forced to walk down a long corridor. "Then there's a black, glazed partition that he starts to see Irma's shadow through," says assistant art director James Spencer. "He eventually makes it to her room, and when he opens the door, it's filled with all these fabrics. This tells the story of who she is and what she does. He makes his way through and eventually sees Irma there, and she's not quite what he expected."

A FRENCH DELIGHT

Set decorator Anna Pinnock really enjoyed dressing Irma's attic space. "I don't think I came out of that set for five days solid," she remembers. "Everything in that set came from France. And the most fantastic thing was that the actress playing Irma, Danielle Hugues, who is French, came in and just threw herself on the bed, a bit like a child does when they love to get into a place, and said, 'This is so French. I just feel this is France.'" It was a proud moment for Anna. "That was fantastic for me, because that's what you do it for, isn't it, to get that good feedback?"

HOGWARTS 1927

Theseus, Leta, and other Ministry of Magic personnel visit Hogwarts to interview Dumbledore regarding what he knows about Grindelwald and Credence. "Returning to Hogwarts is like returning home, in a way," says executive producer Tim Lewis. For several scenes, and for the first time since shooting the Harry Potter films, the production team returned to Lacock Abbey to film in the familiar cloisters. "I think it's nice from an audience's point of view that we are able to bring in places that we knew from before," Tim continues. "And fortunately, those places still exist."

A GOLDEN AGE

There was no need to "age" anything for Hogwarts in 1927. "Hogwarts is centuries old," explains assistant art director James Spencer. "So in the relative time from when Dumbledore was young and teaching there to when Harry Potter was there, not a lot would change, because it's such an old, established place. The uniforms are slightly different, but the architecture is the same."

TEACHER TO STUDENT

"We see Dumbledore through the eyes of Newt Scamander, who is a man apart from politics," says screenwriter J.K. Rowling. "And we learn that he was a great teacher, but he's a man who doesn't appear to tell anyone the whole truth. He's a man who is burdened with knowledge. You know, it's not easy being Dumbledore," she continues. "He often has information he can't share—he is often swimming against the crowd."

When Auror Torquil Travers asks Dumbledore if he's familiar with *The Predictions of Tycho Dodonus*, Dumbledore replies that he is. He's also aware that Travers wants something from him. But even though Dumbledore says he is doing what he can to stop Grindelwald's plans, he will not actively fight him. Consequently, Travers does not accept that Dumbledore is on their side.

DRESSING HOGWARTS 1927

In filmic terms, designers can "dress" not just actors but also sets and locations. Many props and set dressings had been saved from the eight Harry Potter films, with a good many displayed at the Warner Bros. Studio Tour at Leavesden. Even though it was fairly easy to go "next door" and bring something back to use, creating Hogwarts in a different era required a combination of previously seen and new items, not the least of which was the castle itself!

TECH SCHOOL

Because much of the physical Hogwarts set was destroyed in *Harry Potter and the Deathly Hallows – Part 2*, the production for *Fantastic Beasts: The Crimes of Grindelwald* used the digital version of Hogwarts. "We built quite a piece of the viaduct and some of the tower," says Martin Foley, "but they reconstructed the castle from the digital model we created for the last few films."

BACK IN SERVICE

The desks used in the Harry Potter films were taken out of storage and used in the 1927 Hogwarts classrooms. Students did carry "new" schoolbooks, although these didn't require the usual detailed work from the graphics department, as they were on screen for only fleeting moments. One of the biggest differences in the students' supplies was that they used satchels impressed with the Hogwarts crest instead of the shoulder-hanging rucksacks used in the 2000s.

OLD-SCHOOL TIES

The Hogwarts uniforms of 1927 have some notable differences from those of the Harry Potter era. "The gowns for Harry Potter were black, and these are a dark blue," says costume supervisor Charlotte Finlay. New details have been added, including three velvet stripes on the bell of the sleeve, and the house colors line only the interior of the hood, which has wider lapels. The designer and the design of the robes might be different, but the costume department used the same company who manufactured the robes for the Harry Potter films to supply the 1927 versions.

DUMBLEDORE'S DEFENSE AGAINST THE DARK ARTS CLASS

In 1927, Albus Dumbledore (portrayed by Jude Law) was the Defense Against the Dark Arts professor and much beloved among the students. Director David Yates and costume designer Colleen Atwood had several conversations about what *this* Dumbledore was like. "We wanted him to be young and hopeful," she says. "The professor that the kids all loved, the guy who was their go-to guy. Outsiders connected with him and the cool kids connected with him, because he was approachable." In one scene, Dumbledore is teaching a familiar lesson to his students—using the *Riddikulus!* spell to counteract their personal Boggarts.

IN A CLASS OF ONE'S OWN

Both of Jude Law's parents are teachers, so he enjoyed being "teacher for a day." "David Yates made the whole shooting of that scene really feel like a class," he says. "The children were thrilled to be in these familiar surroundings." Jude admits that he did have a strange experience while shooting the scene. "I've watched those classes like everyone else, and to be in it was, as it sometimes is in acting, somewhat 'out of body.' You're in there doing it, but then you look back at yourself and realize how special it was."

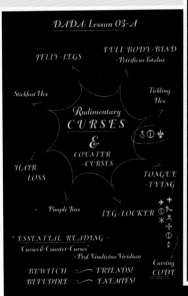

DADA: Lesson 03-A

JELLY-LEGS   FULL BODY-BIND
             - Petrificus Totalus

Stickfast Hex   Tickling
                        Hex

        Rudimentary
          CURSES
             &
          COUNTER
          -CURSES

HAIR
LOSS   TONGUE
                        -TYING

  Pimple Jinx   LEG-LOCKER

· ESSENTIAL READING -
'Curses & Counter-Curses'
    - Prof. Vindictus Viridian
                        Cursing
                         CODE
BEWITCH   FRIENDS!
BEFUDDLE   ENEMIES!

DADA: Lesson 12.5

Essential BOGGART
      DEFENCE

· HOW to detect a Boggart
   Recognised signs... - Scratching
              - Rattling, Shaking

Riddikulus   YES   No
(⚕⚖⚗⚘⚙⚚⚛ →)
              Defence Charm
FORCE OF MIND   RAT
Make fun of boggart   - Rattus
= dispelled in
amusement!   FEAR

· WHERE do Boggarts hide?
              CUPBOARDS
   Tea-pots Desks
   CONFINED SPACES
Caves /   (& DARK!)   · Rare sightings
woodland   by MUGGLES!

SEEING STARS

Each Defense Against the Dark Arts professor has a classroom influenced by their own personality or interests. For Dumbledore, his interest in astronomy was highlighted. Pieces from the future headmaster's office had to be taken out of storage and "un-aged." A mechanical model of the solar system, called an *orrery*, from *Harry Potter and the Chamber of Secrets* was reconstructed by its original prop makers, Terry Whitehouse and John Blakeley. "We fired it up again, and it all worked, all the planets went around," says Terry. "It was like having an old friend back."

New items for Dumbledore's Defense Against the Dark Arts classroom include a fifteen-foot telescope built by Pierre Bohanna and a moon-shaped globe that hangs from the ceiling. The moon was made of metal, and craters and lines were etched onto its surface.

MEMORIES: NEWT AND LETA

While at Hogwarts, Leta Lestrange takes a turn around the school, remembering her time as a student and her relationship with Newt Scamander. "Everybody assumes that because she's a Lestrange, Leta is bad," says David Heyman. "She *has* acted out and done bad, sometimes terrible things in the past. But she's also a decent person. She's wrestling with what is expected of her and who she really is."

IN A CUPBOARD UNDER THE STAIRS

The screenplay described a private area for Newt at Hogwarts as a cupboard. "It's quite a generous cupboard," says Stuart Craig. "It's a secret place where he nurtures and tends strange little creatures. Compared with his later adventures, these are quite modest in size." The cupboard contains brooms and other cleaning supplies, but then a spiral staircase leads up to a large window between flying buttresses where Newt has made an area on the windowsill.

CREATURE COMFORT

"There's a moment in this film [when] you see Newt in Hogwarts in his tiny cupboard menagerie and Leta accidentally barges in," says Eddie Redmayne. "Newt is trying to heal a damaged raven chick, and Leta asks, 'Why do you care about that?' He replies, 'Well, because it's hurt.' Newt has such empathy for anything or anyone that is hurt. And what he's best at is helping."

BE LOVED

"On paper, their friendship might not make sense," says Zoë Kravitz, "but Newt loves the things that no one else will love, and Leta *is* that in a lot of ways. He's the only person who really sees her for who she is, and she needs that in her life."

Before Leta leaves Hogwarts, she meets up with Dumbledore, who expresses sympathy that rumors of her lost brother have been brought up again.

NICOLAS FLAMEL

During their visit on the dome of St. Paul's in London, Dumbledore gives Newt a business card for a safe house in Paris. Newt Apparates, with Tina, Jacob, and Kama, to the address on the card so that he can settle the Zouwu in his case and figure out next steps. After Tina and Newt leave, Jacob is greeted by the owner of the house: Nicolas Flamel, the six-hundred-year-old alchemist who is the only known maker of the Sorcerer's Stone. Flamel isn't surprised at their arrival. In fact, Dumbledore had told him they would drop by.

WORD OF HONOR

Actor Brontis Jodorowsky calls playing Nicolas Flamel a "great privilege. First, he's a well-known character for fans of the Harry Potter story. And second, everybody knows he's a very close friend of Dumbledore. So I really felt it was a privilege and a responsibility to give life to this character in a way that will be both appealing for the public for what they're expecting, but also bring some little surprises, like what is a six-hundred-year-old man doing in this story?"

AGING FOR HOURS

Brontis endured up to four hours in the makeup chair while prostheses were applied to age him. "It's a long process where little by little you're erasing yourself and allowing the character to come," he says. "You really change your face, you have the wig; even your hands are aged."

OLD SCHOOL

How do you play the part of a six-hundred-year-old man? It's not like you have someone to interview about it. "I read about alchemy," says Brontis. "I read about him. I made my research a basis for the character, but you're not supposed to perform your studies, right?" Brontis admits it's impossible to know what it is like to be six hundred years old, but he also points out that the Sorcerer's Stone might have aged Flamel differently than we expect.

Inside Flamel's Home

Nicolas Flamel's house seems to be about the same age as he is. "We made a half-timbered house," says Stuart Craig, "which we would call Tudor style in the UK. So it's very different from the buildings surrounding it." Nicolas Flamel was a real alchemist who lived in Paris in the fourteenth and fifteenth centuries, and his house at 51 rue de Montmorency is still there.

TIME WARP

Stuart Craig truly enjoyed designing and building Flamel's house. "It has such character of great antiquity," says Stuart. "The place is absolutely crowded, and the timbers are actually rotting." All the floors have curved over the years, and the stairs are leaning. The construction crew needed to make it look as if the walls and beams were bent and warped. "Everything has twisted as time has carried on," says Martin Foley.

PROPS TO THE PROPS

Just as he had created the flasks and tubes for Potions classes, Pierre Bohanna created the lab equipment for Flamel's alchemical work. "We're really gobsmacked at his ingenuity," says Stuart Craig. "He is an amazing engineer, sometimes on a really minute scale. Some days he's like a watchmaker, and on others, he's like an engineer designing bridges."

Flamel also has a large crystal ball. When Jacob asks if it can show him Queenie, it shows her heading to the Lestrange family cemetery, and Jacob runs off to find her.

A MAGICAL TOME

Flamel uses a thick magical tome to communicate with an elite association of wizards. "Inside, it looks like a photo album," says Eduardo Lima, "with moving images of the different wizards' work areas." "It's like a WhatsApp group," says Miraphora Mina with a laugh.

THE SORCERER'S STONE

As Harry Potter fans will know, Flamel is in possession of the Sorcerer's Stone, which has made him immortal. "Seventeen years later, we're getting it out again and blowing the dust off," says Pierre Bohanna. Actually, the stone was remade for the Fantastic Beasts film but was cast from the original master mold.

FANTASTIC WANDS

New witches and wizards in *Fantastic Beasts: The Crimes of Grindelwald* means new wands. "A wand is many things," says Pierre Bohanna, head of the modeling department, "but it's also a piece of style. They're very bespoke to the character."

THESEUS SCAMANDER

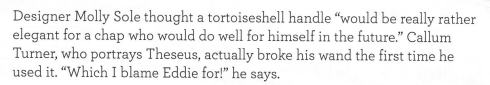

Designer Molly Sole thought a tortoiseshell handle "would be really rather elegant for a chap who would do well for himself in the future." Callum Turner, who portrays Theseus, actually broke his wand the first time he used it. "Which I blame Eddie for!" he says.

LETA LESTRANGE

The prop makers wanted Leta's wand to be feminine but powerful-looking. Molly Sole chose ebony for the wand stem, as "Leta also has a strong pure-blood family background, and we wanted the wand to reflect that level of prestige. It had to look rich and commanding."

BUNTY

"Bunty is this really sweet character who's obsessed with animals and in touch with nature," says Molly Sole about Newt's assistant, "so I thought a fir cone would make a really nice handle and I put on a design of little ivy leaves wrapping around the wood."

ALBUS DUMBLEDORE

The shaft of Dumbledore's ebony wand displays a braided section that tapers to a long, smooth tip. The wand is "formal and elegant and restrained," says designer Molly Sole. "The twisted stem, left close to its natural organic shape, is a nod to Dumbledore's maverick, self-confident nature." A silver collar divides the handle from the shaft, which is etched with runes that represent Dumbledore's initials in Runic writing and that invoke wisdom, justice, and strength. Jude Law studied the wand moves of his predecessors in the role, in addition to orchestra conductors and even a film of Pablo Picasso painting, to develop his own style of wand work.

NICOLAS FLAMEL

Nicolas Flamel is six hundred years old, so the designers wanted something that looked ancient. Molly Sole was inspired by a very old horse whip with a bone end that her mother had collected. "I always thought it would make a really fantastic wand handle," says Molly. The wand has a faux-bone handgrip with a gold joiner that connects to a mahogany shaft.

JACOB KOWALSKI

"Wouldn't it be amazing if someone handed me a wand at some point and said, 'Here, hold this,' and then I did something with it?" says Dan Fogler. "I do a lot of leaning back so I don't get hit by the energies coming out of the wands. That's basically my relationship with wands, which is sad, but you know, I'm magic on the inside and I've got a soul of gold."

PERSONAL STYLE

Bohanna continues, "[Wands] want to reflect not just the character's personality but also their taste and their influences and what they like and don't like. And so to take that principle, it's actually almost liberating. It gives out a little set of rules for the designers to work with, interpret, and riff off of, really."

YUSUF KAMA

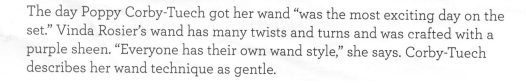

Yusuf Kama's wand has an ebony handle and a partridge shaft, separated by a silver cuff, with a silver band at the hilt end.

VINDA ROSIER

The day Poppy Corby-Tuech got her wand "was the most exciting day on the set." Vinda Rosier's wand has many twists and turns and was crafted with a purple sheen. "Everyone has their own wand style," she says. Corby-Tuech describes her wand technique as gentle.

ABERNATHY

The handle of Abernathy's wand is ebony and is separated from the shaft by a silver cuff. "In terms of Abernathy's ability to deliver and execute a spell, it's very much like him," says Kevin Guthrie. "Simple and to the point. There's nothing wishy-washy or flashy. It's direct and it's quite targeted, I would say. He's very much a character who's told who to take out and is able to deliver on that. So it's specific and neat."

KRALL

The wand of Krall, an acolyte of Grindelwald, has a silver tip.

CARROW

Grindelwald's acolyte Carrow wields a plain, baton-style wand.

GUNNAR GRIMMSON

For the bounty hunter Grimmson's wand, Stuart Craig had the idea that it would be an old piece of knotted, gnarly wood. "Really rough and almost hand-whittled, with whorls on it. It's a workman-like tool, and he's also carved mementos of his kills into it," says Molly Sole. "They're like a sign for him, what he's managed to achieve. I think he really cares about getting one-up on Newt, and it's probably his way of saying, right, I've done this and I've done that."

RUDOLPH SPIELMAN

Head of Incarceration for the International Confederation of Wizards, Rudolph Spielman has an ebony wand with an ivory handle and an inlaid silver design.

SKENDER

Circus Arcanus owner Skender's wand reflects his big-top vocation, with a large red ball top and a pennant-like design that encircles the handle. The light wood of the wand is dirty and scratched.

INSIDE THE MINISTÈRE DES AFFAIRES MAGIQUES RECORDS ROOM

During their secret meeting in London, Dumbledore tells Newt about a box hidden in the French ministry's Records Room, which houses the deeds belonging to all pure-blood wizarding families. There he should be able to locate information on Credence's identity. In order to get into the ministry, Newt drinks Polyjuice Potion to turn himself into his brother, Theseus.

TOWERING STYLE

The Records Room is a stunning example of Art Nouveau design. "The towers in the Records Room were described in the script as being tall, grown elements, like trees," says art director Sam Leake. The towers are embellished with twisting floral designs and ribbon shapes, true to the Art Nouveau style.

The towers in the Records Room resemble bombé-style French furniture, so named because their curves bulge outward in the front.

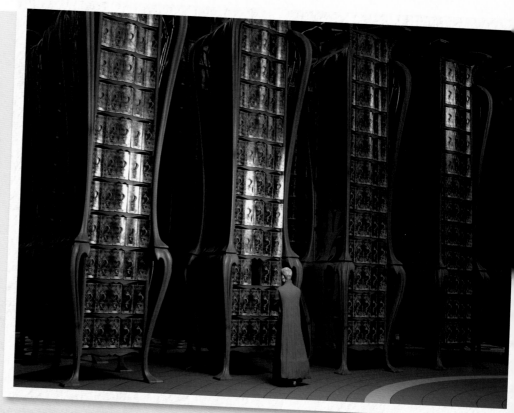

ALL FOR ONE

"There were over a thousand massive deed boxes to create," says supervising prop modeler Terry Whitehouse, "so we sent up a flare for help." Each box had a handle glued on and then needed to be painted and aged. "It was a hard slog, but it often happens that you need to drop what you're doing to help with other jobs," added Whitehouse.

THE LESTRANGE FAMILY TREE

The artwork of the Lestrange family tree brings to mind the tapestry illustrating the Noble House of Black in *Harry Potter and the Order of the Phoenix*. In fact, the Lestrange family tree was created by Miraphora Mina, who also created the Black tapestry. "We didn't know the whole backstory, so, again, like the tapestry in *Order of the Phoenix*, we had to ask Jo [Rowling] for the names for the actual tree." The screenwriter gave her one side of the family, "but, of course, a tree needs a bit more. So I had to make up the other side. And they all married cousins," she reveals.

Once in the Records Room, Tina finally learns that Newt was never engaged to Leta and that his heart belongs to her.

Escape from the Records Room

As Newt and Tina try to locate the right deed box, Leta shows up. Leta, it turns out, is looking for the same box, which has information about her missing brother that she does not want revealed. Suddenly, the feline Matagots who guard the Ministère appear and threaten them. When Leta starts throwing spells at the beasts, they become even more aggressive and attack Newt and Tina.

RÉALITÉ VIRTUELLE

The Records Room, with its flying towers, is reminiscent of the Hall of Prophecy at the Ministry of Magic with its endless shelves, so the filmmakers employed the same virtual approach they used in *Harry Potter and the Order of the Phoenix*. "There were lots of green-screened props for the actors to dodge and interact with, but it's basically a full CG environment," Tim Burke explains. The scene was developed in pre-vis before many rehearsals to finalize the action.

EVERY TRICK IN THE BOOKCASE

Several "types" of bookcases were designed for the Records Room action sequence: green-screen-wrapped bases that could move up, down, and sideways; bookcases that rotated; and a remote-controlled bookcase that could be driven in any direction.

When the Lestrange record box is finally located, Leta finds that the records are missing. Inside there's only a note saying the records have been taken to the Lestrange family mausoleum.

UNUSUAL TRANSPORTATION

While in Newt's case, the Zouwu is able to recover from its wounds. So Newt releases it and rides on its back with Tina and Leta, who are now in the case. They head to the cemetery where the Lestrange family members are buried. "The puppeteers crafted this extraordinary, bucking bronco–type of engineering," says Eddie Redmayne, "which had four men dressed in full-on green morph suits moving it around."

SUMMONED TO THE CEMETERY

Newt, Tina, and Leta arrive at the Lestrange mausoleum, where Grindelwald has arranged a rally to convey his ideas and recruit new supporters. Among the crowd of wizards and witches are some familiar faces: Credence and the Maledictus, Kama, and Jacob, who has finally reunited with Queenie.

A TOUCHING MOMENT

When the Zouwu drops Newt, Tina, and Leta at the cemetery, we witness an affectionate moment between the Magizoologist and the beast he has rescued. The Zouwu gives Newt a friendly lick and a hug before going back into the case. The puppeteers sculpted a Zouwu head made of very soft foam. "It could be touched and pushed," says Robin Guiver, "so once Eddie gets off the stunt rig he rides on, he can have that physical interaction." "This is one of the most surreal days of work I've ever had," says Eddie Redmayne, "and you always end up with the weirdest pains from muscles that you didn't know existed!"

THE LESTRANGE MAUSOLEUM

"Our first entry point is in the Lestrange family mausoleum," says Stuart Craig, "where the coffins of deceased Lestranges are on the shelves of their crypt. From there you go downstairs into the amphitheater, where Grindelwald will be holding his rally."

FROM THE GROUND UP

The production crew researched the Père Lachaise Cemetery in Paris, which was built in the 1600s. "It's set up on a hill," says Martin Foley, "and there are areas where it's almost like an amphitheater of tombs around you." This was inspirational, as all the story elements would resolve at the rally held in a large-scale underground amphitheater.

THE GRAVEYARD SHIFT

The production actually filmed at Highgate Cemetery in north London for a few nights. "It was great to be out on location," says Martin Foley, "and spooky being in a real cemetery, but the crew enjoyed it. Then the weather took a turn for the worse, and we had two more days of shooting yet, so we built it in the studio to finish the scenes."

RALLY IN THE AMPHITHEATER

As Grindelwald prepares to address his old and new followers at the rally, Queenie asks Jacob to keep an open mind. She is interested in Grindelwald's cause, as he has promised her that, under his revolution, she will be able to marry Jacob.

RISING TO THE OCCASION

"There are a lot of underground elements in the film, because the wizards' world is still underground," says Martin Foley. "That's the point. Grindelwald is trying to bring everyone out of secrecy, so this felt like a good setting. But Stuart Craig doesn't do anything halfway, so when you ask for an amphitheater, you get a four-thousand-person-capacity amphitheater!"

The Lestrange family symbol is a raven, so thirteen ten-foot-tall ravens hold the amphitheater roof up with their wings. One master raven was handsculpted, then molded and cast twelve more times.

ON THE FACE OF IT

Colleen Atwood was tasked with creating costumes and assigning them to the extras who are the rally's attendants. "What I looked for was a 'face,'" she explains. "As a man came in, I would see something in his face that I felt could become a businessman who's gone astray or a disheartened worker. It was a time of huge turmoil." When it came to the women, Colleen took the advice of David Yates. "'Think of it like a rock concert,' he said to me, so I felt as if they were groupies." And Colleen recognized that fans, like groupies, often try to dress like the people they're watching onstage. "They all take a nod from Grindelwald."

CHOICES

As the rally culminates, choices must be made. Who will follow Grindelwald? And who will fight?

ANSWERING THE CALL

"What I consciously wanted was to have this gallery of people whose backstories we understand," explains J.K. Rowling. "We get to know their personal struggles, biases, and traumas, and in the middle of it we have Grindelwald. Now, which of these characters will hear his siren call? The individual stories culminate in the rally that Grindelwald holds, where all these characters with their diverse histories, their diverse blood statuses, their own preoccupations, find themselves in this auditorium facing this man. Is he the answer? And for some of these characters he is—or seems to be."

FAMILIAR BEGINNINGS

"Jo [Rowling] has taken the characters that she introduced us to in the first Fantastic Beasts film and is showing how they are woven into the lore of the Potter series," says Eddie Redmayne. "You get to meet these people at a different stage in their lives. We're seeing them when the stakes were different but still incredibly high. So for me, this film has a depth and a rooted darkness to it, but also a newfound familiarity that I love."

THE POTTER CONNECTION

As J.K. Rowling explains, the Harry Potter and Fantastic Beasts franchises are connected through the characters. "You stumble across quite a few people and places and things that you'll recognize. At the same time, though, I'm telling a discrete story within the Fantastic Beasts franchise that is only hinted at in the Potter books, which is the rise of Grindelwald, who was a wizard who seriously threatened the security of the wizarding and the larger world, and his antagonist, Dumbledore, who, of course, is a key character in the Potter books. This was backstory that I always had lots of ideas about, and now I get to tell it, which is artistically really satisfying."

Copyright © 2018 Warner Bros. Entertainment Inc. FANTASTIC
BEASTS: THE CRIMES OF GRINDELWALD characters, names
and related indicia are © & ™ Warner Bros. Entertainment Inc.
WB SHIELD: © & ™ WBEI. WIZARDING WORLD trademark
and logo © & ™ Warner Bros. Entertainment Inc. Publishing
Rights © JKR. (s18)

All rights reserved. No part of this book may be reproduced,
transmitted, or stored in an information retrieval system in
any form or by any means, graphic, electronic, or mechanical,
including photocopying, taping, and recording, without prior
written permission from the publisher.

ISBN: 978-0-241-36701-8

Published in the United States by Random House Children's
Books, a division of Penguin Random House LLC, 1745
Broadway, New York, NY 10019, and in Canada by Penguin
Random House Canada Limited, Toronto. Random House and
the colophon are registered trademarks of Penguin Random
House LLC. Published in Great Britain by Penguin Books 2018.

www.penguin.co.uk

MANUFACTURED IN CHINA

10 9 8 7 6 5 4 3 2 1

PRODUCED BY:

PO Box 3088
San Rafael, CA 94912
www.insighteditions.com

Publisher: Raoul Goff
Associate Publisher: Vanessa Lopez
Creative Director: Chrissy Kwasnik
Designer: Evelyn Furuta
Editor: Greg Solano
Editorial Assistant: Hilary VandenBroek
Senior Production Editor: Rachel Anderson
Production Direction/Subsidiary Rights: Lina s Palma
Production Manager: Greg Steffen

ROOTS of PEACE   REPLANTED PAPER

Insight Editions, in association with Roots of Peace, will plant two trees
for each tree used in the manufacturing of this book. Roots of Peace is
an internationally renowned humanitarian organization dedicated to
eradicating land mines worldwide and converting war-torn lands into
productive farms and wildlife habitats. Roots of Peace will plant two
million fruit and nut trees in Afghanistan and provide farmers there with
the skills and support necessary for sustainable land use.